LIFE ON MY BREATH

LIFE ON MY BREATH

David Zeiger

SARNA PRESS

ACKNOWLEDGMENTS

Thanks to the editors of the following magazines and anthologies in which these poems were first published:

COLLEGE ENGLISH, XANADU, GREEN FUSE, MINNESOTA REVIEW, TELEPHONE, THE LITERARY REVIEW, FREE LUNCH, WEST HILLS REVIEW, POETS ON:, VISIONS, MANHATTAN POETRY REVIEW, BLUE UNICORN, MICKLE STREET REVIEW, HOME PLANET NEWS, CONFRONTATION, NEW YORK QUARTERLY, POEM, CEDARMERE REVIEW, ESPRIT, GYPSY, OKTOBERFEST, SLANT, VERVE, CONNECTICUT RIVER REVIEW, WORDSMITH, THE CATHARTIC, EAST WEST, WINDLESS ORCHARD, SALOME, and the following anthologies: MIXED VOICES (Milkweed Editions), SCARECROW POETRY (Ashland Poetry Press), WE SPEAK FOR PEACE (KIT Trends Inc.)

PUBLISHED BY
SARNA PRESS
9 FOURTH RD.
GREAT NECK, NY 11021

Library of Congress Catalog Card Number: 94-69982

ISBN 0-9644763-0-4

Produced at The Print Center, Inc., 225 Varick St., New York, NY 10014, a non-profit facility for literary and arts-related publications. (212) 206-8465

CONTENTS

For Lila

I
PROLOGUES
TO ARRIVAL

LIFE ON MY BREATH

Needing
to taste life on my breath
at twelve,
I sliced a peeling cylinder
of onion
laying bare each petal of flesh,
pale, thin mirror of my own,
arranged them on slabs
of seeded corn bread
buttered thick
and devoured them
through comforting tears,
embracing the knife
in the nasal passages.

The fire on my breath
stayed the day
lighting up the winter dark.
Needing
to nourish my hungers
the onion and I were intimate
as lovers,
the fire smell entering
my bones.

AT POOL SIDE

Sitting at pool side
watching the manly men promenade
in their brief tank suits,
pelvic bulges like medals,
I say to myself
If I were born in my scrawny body again
neurasthenic nervous system and all
(having survived spinal meningitis,
outlasted three brothers,
endured the consolation
of nervous women)
I'd go off the high board.
I would be less careful.

CONEY ISLAND SUMMER

is my hell's furnace.
I cannot take the sun.
I sit up through nights
alone, a spindly child
with vinegar-soaked sheets
on blistered shoulders and back,
lips quivering.

How to tell her
standing there
at surf's edge, buxom, tanned,
I sit beneath
the boardwalk slats,
the sun starting up again.
How to say her dark
draws the light from my eyes
her ocean
gray breakers of pain.

In our furnished room
bleached by sea air
she hopes to fatten me
feeding me sweet cream.

(Sand in everything, everywhere.)

On Friday, late, Poppa came
red-haired, freckled fair,
slid in her arms till daylight,
romped in the noon-day waves
his touch like shade,
left Sunday night
burned.
Noxzema's smell still sickens me.

We were never the flesh
of her dream.

COMMUTER

Stumbling down the aisle of the smoking car
on the way to New York
half awake in the stale haze,
I am suddenly six again
rocking to market on my father's horse and wagon
half awake in the ripening dawn,
seated beside him with shivering lips,
swaying gently in the clear wind.
I steal glances at his smoky breath,
his unshaven face terse in shadow,
the early mist lifting to the clip-clop
of the universe.
A sudden lurch.
I fall toward the card players
at the end of the car intent
on the pinochle game on the attaché case.
My father's hand round my waist to steady me.
With the other, he holds lightly the reins.
I pull desperately with all my strength
on the handle of the door
to pass through.
The effort brings me close to tears.

TO THE STATION

Walking to the railroad station
private in the green of morning
and the grass already awake,
I swing past polished lawns
and flagstone walks
in perfect focus.

Young executives on bicycles
pass me by,
attaché cases behind them,
while silver women chauffeur
husbands to our mustering point.

At varying rates of speed
we converge on the station
knowing
that what we have left behind
will prosper
with the ordinary drift of day.
What lies ahead
we can contain with cunning.

POEM FOR THE FOURTH OF JULY

"America, the plum blossoms are falling.
My mind is made up, there's going to be trouble."
—Allen Ginsberg

Son of an immigrant presser, I celebrate
the holiday at the beach, hot dogs & knishes,
throw up on the roller coaster
and crawl back on the BMT to my ghetto.

A five-year old in high button shoes
starting school in Brownsville without English,
pledging allegiance to the republic
for "Richard Stands, one nation invisible," I come

from streets lined with pushcarts, peddlers
jostling each other, singing, swearing, shouting
in foreign tongues, time slipping away
like food, like spilling pollen.

Tonight, I'm a suburbanite standing shoulder
to shoulder with the crowd in Morgan Park
far from the blood in crumbling inner cities,
watching neon flowers flare in the black sky.

Far from Brownsville, planet of crack,
AIDS, and sudden death, I consider
my several lives and the place of memory
in a time of swelling doubt.

One foot still in Brownsville,
the other on a suburban walk
in a shopping mall, slipping
on a condom floating in spilled beer.

FOR MY BIRTHDAY

my daughter gives me
a personal capsule of history
from Library of Congress archives—
an original issue of The New York Times
published the day I was born.

Yellow with age,
edges brittle and crumbling—
metaphor for my self?—
I lift it gently from the clear
vinyl envelope enclosed
in leather folder No. 123668
to read the world I was entering:

HARDING ASSUMES LEADERSHIP AS CONGRESS LAGS
RUSSIA ARMS FOR WAR AS MILLIONS STARVE
8 DROWNINGS MAR DAY FOR BATHERS.
On the day I am born, local thunder showers
are forecast to greet my arrival.
Three-piece Men's Suits sell at Iverson & Heneage
for forty-six dollars
and Fiorello LaGuardia gets set to run
on a five-cent fare platform plank.

Selling for two cents in Greater NY,
four cents elsewhere, pinched words
in narrow columns
speak decorously
in hushed tones.

On the day I am born
a jealous lover shoots his rival
and hangs himself.
A man angered by a trolley
smashes the car door

and two youths are arrested
for killing an 85-year old woman.

Special Care Instructions warn me
to keep these pages from the light
as they are "highly subject
to deterioration from exposure
to atmospheric conditions."
At risk of flaking away the rest,
I explore no further, replacing the sheets
in their plastic shell, fragments
peeling away at every motion.
The sound of time drifts in mist.
I exist. The world burns. Over
and over it happens.

HONDA FREE

For instance,
our new two-door Honda, silver LX Accord
as statement to the world
our parents dead, our children grown.
For instance,
remaking ourselves
sunk
in red plush buckets
whizzing along
smooth
to accelerating hum
small people in, tall people out
barreling through traffic racing
past station wagons loaded
with kids and gear
past lumbering tractor-trailers, vans
pressing
our small silver bird
propelled by wind.
Resolute, vulnerable,
we have never been younger
than this.

SO FAR

it's touch and go.
Midnight.
Unreeling down the Expressway
in the left lane
doing sixty
hands frozen to the wheel.
Guerrillas zig-zag in and out.
It's touch and go.
Abandoned wrecks, tail-pipes,
tires in moonscape
edge the road.
Riveted to tail-lights ahead
I scan the rear-view mirror
for danger,
comb the dark out there
for warnings, tensed
to brake.

You sleep beside me
anaesthetized
in yellow light,
your face tilted
in this windy space,
a tiny engine against
the universe.

Later in bed
you shake me awake.
Broken moans.
A billowing hearse lurches
toward me,
black coach careening
chauffeur-less.
A loved one dead?
A random killing
without remorse?
It's touch and go.

IF I FORGET THEE

If I forget thee, O Jerusalem,
standing here on the ledge of Abu Tour
among the chartered buses and souvenir peddlers
looking west to the Wall, the Mosque, the Basilica,

while Arabs place kaffiyehs on squealing tourists,
hoist them onto camels for two dollars a head—
if I remember thee not,
let my Nikon forget its cunning.

Here, in the City of David
I have returned from my diaspora
bundled and greased against the sun,
my tongue cleaving to the roof of my mouth

even as I recall yesterday's climb
into the Judean hills,
oleander and hibiscus blossoms
among the trucks left by the roadside.

On this, the day of my chiefest joy,
a Satmar Chasid in caftan, beard, and earlocks
told me the State of Israel does not exist
as the Messiah has not yet come.

CLASSIC FACT OR FANCY

In a dark kitchen rent by lightning,
my mother, eyes wild, pursues me
with a cat o'nine tails
because I won't finish my lumpy oatmeal.

Squashed between giants
at my brother's graveside,
I drift between grief and indifference
trying to understand the words
intoned under the grey sky.

My first-grade teacher
questions the welts on my arms,
her face becomes a death's head
stealing my voice
as the class giggles.

Chased by wild dogs,
I scream multiplication tables
hoping to turn them away.

One day last week,
lost in small talk,
I entered the co-ed pool area
without my suit,
bridging the abyss between nightmare
and reality.
I told myself I dreamt it.
A red flag
in the shifting landscape
of sanity.

How comforting
that what I remember
didn't happen.

IN TRANSIT

Schoolboy hobo beyond Mama's grasp
in the back of a pick-up
bumping across the postcard face of Vermont
on Interstate 91 headed for Canada.

Legs flapping on the tailgate,
drunk on pine smell,
scrawny body rocking in green wind,
he's run off with a strep throat.
Can't swallow.

At Newport's border, the infirmary
of granite-towered St. Mary's of the Sea,
nuns invite him to stay overnight.
He begs off, sleepless with new world imagery.

They feed him liquids, fill his pockets
with sulfa pills, wish him Godspeed.
He staggers out the gate.

Three days and whole again, he wanders
back alleys of Quebec.
A girl in white takes his hand
leading him to her cell bed
lit by candlelight.
They sit and talk in halting French.
"Why?" he asks.

Impatience knits her brow.
All business for the core of things,
she shoves him into the dingy street.
Washed in cool flood of night,
he breathes a new universe
loud with silence.
Specks of light quiver overhead.

CLIMBING MT. WASHINGTON

Two thousand feet above treeline now
crouched on a ledge jagged as my heartbeat
in this wind from another planet
I undo my pack to get at quick-energy raisins
and Hershey bar,
studying the drift of mist and shadow
on the ridges below.
On the Appalachian Mt. bag
the guidelines for wilderness hikers
are green on white:
"Mountain weather is unpredictable"
"Mountain mishaps are rare, but..."
Yesterday, a helicopter lifted from these glacial rocks
a climber,
both legs broken.

Each step here at earth's edge is a death wish,
but I must believe what I have come to know
at fifty-five
of old bones caught in the lifting tide of will,
of the frivolity of balance.

The young, sturdy and sure-footed, pass me by.

Later, I will crawl around the yellow cairns
at my own pace to the summit
where the tourists come by car and rail
to buy picture postcards at the souvenir shop
near the weather station,
then peer down on tilted fields of stone.

GETTING BY

Poking through garbage in trash cans
somehow brings back childhood visions
of pickles in brine floating deep
in wooden barrels. Then too we
built fires to warm frozen fingers
as we hunched over the pushcarts.
We lived with hope then, shoring up
our careless strength against this time.
The pundits' words were like rumbles
of thunder on hot summer days
beyond the passive horizon.
Last night I killed a man who took
my wood from the lean-to. He was
skin and bones, but he pulled a knife.
Now I must rest before I go
to the water hole. Teeth will be
bared, and the strongest will drink first.

THE EXHIBIT

Visitors to the tiny toilet off the side entrance
to our house
encounter small objets d'art on walls
at eye-level when they sit,
sepia snapshots scattered among small mirrors
in chintzy frames,
painted Lilliputian plaster birds,
metal logos in script from Ford and Chevrolet,
baroque bottle openers, emblems, coins, mini-sculptures,
each with its own color and voice.

In the snapshots,
how we do not smile
in our white stockings and high-buttoned shoes.
This one to the left
shows you already incandescent
in your mother's arms as she turns you
full-face to the camera.
I stare at you from the opposite wall
posed on a kitchen chair,
world-weary sober in Buster Brown haircut
and kneepants three sizes too large.
A miniature brass hand
spans the distance between prints
of me as six-year old ring boy
in tuxedo and top hat,
and you at five, seated luscious and formal
on a low stool.

Guests tell me
the time spent in this gallery
is never enough beyond its purpose.
The poster on the door
stolen from a Chinese restaurant reads:
"Wash Hands Before Leaving This Room"

EARLY MORNING

Watching you hose the front lawn
in early morning sun
before dazzle
before shadow's hush erases
all possibility of grace,
I know
others like you inhabit other galaxies.
Otherwise, I would mourn.
How your thickening body opens out
over the bed of roses,
some already in rags,
perceiving in them the whole
of everything else,
caressing them with moisture.

Bending to weed,
your liquid presence
floats across the grass.
Curve of neck, wings of small shoulders,
graying hair memorized
through the years
igniting old carnal fires
filling caverns in my head.

The mother air of what you are
bathes the green hedge in love,
quivers like silk
like small stars
we will not see again till dusk.

WALT WHITMAN WALKS MANHATTAN, 1842

The new editor at the New York Aurora,
twenty-three and six-foot slim in black frock coat,
hat and boots, a boutonniere and trimmed beard,
"one of a living crowd" out for a lunchtime stroll
pauses at St. Paul's Chapel to lean on his cane
and scan newspaper row across Broadway,
prodigal eye alive to what has happened,
to what will happen.

Crossing over to Park Row
to avoid the foppery of swells,
he passes the old Park Theatre
recalling "the singers, the tragedians, the comedians"
he loved as teen-age apprentice.
At Nassau St. "discordant notes of the newsboys"
as Walt turns into #162 to work the night,
soon to be sacked because he roars,
won't tone down his leaders.
Having come to measure himself
against the Establishment,
he begins his freedom here,
at the center of the world.

GARDEN TOUR

Ladies straggle down the gravel path
creaming over trillium erectum
seduced by Jack-in-the-Pulpit.
They sniff. They touch.

April muddies the fields.
We slog through endless gardens
interrogating spring:
a dazzle of petal
remaking itself from memory.

I learned to know
a Blue Peter from a rose
only yesterday:
you baptize me
with Latin ritual.

Now
dragging past rhododendron
I remember
the packet of morning-glory seeds
brought home from third grade
my mother dumped
in the garbage.

WAITING

"No one will ever witness extinction,
so we must bear witness to it before the fact."
The Fate of the Earth
—Jonathan Schell

After the voice on the radio reported
we had flung our nuclear bouquet,
the sirens sounded.
I went to my office
and dialed you five times
foundering on the busy signal as always.

Now, shut away from the others,
I listen to an inward song
we heard together once
in the evening of a foreign city
before the contagion of the world drained us,
before we knew nothing could be done,
the tissues of events like tumors.
In the outer corridor, the voices of disbelief,
the clamor of people climbing their fear
as it must have been when clusters of naked Jews
entered the gas vans.

There is nowhere to go.
Thirty miles from here, down the Expressway,
you, too, will turn into your shadow
when the wind enters your eyes,
the tenacity of things melted down
in white light
forever.

POOR RICHARD SAYS

9-year old Danny at classroom front
plays Ben Franklin entering Philadelphia at 17.

God helps those who help themselves, he squeaks,
pale with stage fright, journeying out of himself.

"Think of yourself in a strange city," says Miss Denis,
"Dirty, hungry, no place to sleep." He sees

his big brother, Sam, truant riding the rails to Chicago,
back welted with blood from his father's belt.

The young actor sings out Poor Richard
to the rear desks: *No pains without gains*

and *Little strokes fell great oaks,* his eyes
seeking Sam's face in the back rows.

Ben at 12, is apprenticed to his brother, James, a printer.
Illiterate Sam can't see *Trouble springs from idleness.*

Has never heard of Poor Richard. *He that hath a trade
hath an estate; and he that hath a calling*

hath an office of profit and honor. Danny's Papa
has a trade. Sweatshop presser, little man

with heavy callused hands. What were the hands
of Ben's father like? Soap and candle-maker.

And Ben's hands at 10, when he cut wick
and filled the dipping mold for his father?

Danny has no trade. Hides crying in kitchen corner
watching Sam beaten bloody. *'Tis hard*

for an empty bag to stand upright, says Poor Richard.
Pride is as loud a beggar as want.

Years later, Ben falls out with James.
Danny squanders his youth mourning Sam,

turning back the earth of his early grave.
Poor Richard says, *If you will not hear reason,*

she'll surely rap your knuckles.
They that won't be counselled, can't be helped.

Warped by childhood's windy pain,
Danny lives with always saying goodbye.

Says Poor Richard, *Lost time*
is never found again.

LIFE STORY

The synapse—is that the right word?
grows wider with each year.
The word for yellow clusters
blooming every spring. Proper names
of colleagues "X, Y, and Z" I've known intimately.
Van Gogh's crows over a wheat field.
Munch's scream on the bridge.
Bits and pieces of erosion...broken connection.

At 93, my father was reciting
the Sabbath prayer from memory
when he fell dead.

Coherence is what counts at any age.
The objects aligned at table: plates, napkins,
knives, forks & spoons, salt-shaker.
The give & take with relatives & friends
in familiar landscape while fishing
for the right word.

Was she right to opt out so early
for the Rube Goldberg suicide machine,
the lady—what's her name—
who saw it coming?
Moved from bed to chair, sealed from the past,
from the present, from the calendar.
Is nothingness better?

Add to the porridge—spelled right?—
loss of hearing, struggle with appearances,
the value of hope grows meaningless
like garbled fragments in a foreign tongue.
"Grow old along with me!
The best is yet to be"
passes for art.

Crossword puzzles help, and days
I know "hibiscus" from "begonia"
and how to turn on the CD player.
But, the muted thunder on the horizon:
articulated dread of the empty self.

ORANGES AS THERAPY

We vented our anger on oranges.
We took them from mounded fruit bowls
on kitchen tables,
We lifted them from peddlers' pushcarts,
stole them from the shelves of green-grocers.
In schoolyards, we lobbed them in to each other
at bat, and cheered as
the spheres exploded, citric acid splattering
the infield.
We slid around in the oozing pulp, orange crush
flowing in all directions.
We flung them against brick walls for the thud
and laughed.
We stomped them like Jewish bridegrooms
stomping glass goblets.
The pungent orange smell stayed
in our nostrils.

ELEGY FOR A PRIVATE PERSON
(For M.D.L.)

Just before your sixty-seventh birthday
you arrive at our home in a small cardboard box
marked "PRIORITY MAIL"—Return address:
Evergreen Cemetery & Crematory.

Easy to lift you now. I drive to your apartment,
set you on the oaken chest of drawers
near your bed, leaving you alone
among the rare editions in the glass-enclosed
bookcases, just as you would have wanted,

facing the prints on the wall, the worn rocker,
Tunturi exercycle in the corner.
Every object exudes a funereal pallor
in the cotton silence. Everything
carefully arranged as you left it.

My last night with you, we sat silently
eyeing each other from opposite ends of the room.
An intruder watching you die,
I waited for your secret message,
hoping to strike one spark,
ignite the blurred landscape
of where you were,
but recoiled in fear, knowing just how
you would start to cry.

In the morning, I towelled your bird-thin bones,
dabbed at swollen ankles after the shower,
your privacy trembling as I wondered
how it happened—
the fracture of appetite,

the early dying into singleness.
A life moored only to books.

Weeks ago, you sat bent over Proust
in our living room, sipping weak tea
through a straw, handsome still.
Outside winter was taking hold.
Barren trees darkened
as the cold sun crept past the window
leaving no shadow.

IF I KNEW

this day
were my last   on earth
I'd rise at five and watch
dawn yearn at the window.

I'd lie down with you.
Attend to the music
of your voice.   Scrub away
our angers.
Unplug myself from exercises
pills   the daily paper.
Breakfast
on chocolate mousse cake.
Pursue the rhythm
of my heart.
Light a candle   for those
I've loved   who died.
Gallop my grandson
on my back.
Connect to space   ribbons of wind.
Say yes to losses   weep a little.
Listen to Glenn Gould   play Bach.

Refuse to think about
the enigmatic meaning   of it all.
I'd go down   to the Sound
to the shoreline
to the small waves   angling
into the wind.
Smell   the sunset air
and watch
the colors sprawl   into each other.

ROUTINE

Early Sunday morning, I go out
the front door in pajamas to retrieve
the newspaper flung on the front lawn
and turn around to find a strange house
in the very place where mine stood.
Different shape, color, windows,
curlicued storm door.
Looking around, waiting to wake up,
I am stopped by the county police car
alerted by my strange behavior.
Ashamed to say I can't find my house,
I make small talk.
The cops smirk and drive on.

Our cat's been out all night.
Now, she comes to rub against my leg,
making that throaty hunger sound.
In the deChirico light,
the neighborhood is unfamiliar.
I tremble in the morning chill.
Soon now, very soon, the others will wake,
saunter out to their front lawns.
We can talk.

II
COPING

A VISIT

The whiff of urine—
fallout of the dying and the newly born
floats through open doors
as I stride bright carpets through clusters
of flickering lives
gray with waiting.

At corridor's end
he sits bent,
stiff-jointed and tentative
should some random draft or passion
fill the void.
I break the balance and he turns his head
with a dusty smile.
Together we diagram old wounds,
nibble at bland events
while he recites his litany of ills.

Edging off at last,
I take the old man back
to the plastic plants and chairs of leatherette
where the elevators are
and the ping of the light triggers the kiss
to pry me loose from debt.

TO A RELATIVE BY MARRIAGE

"His place, as he sat and as he thought, was not
In anything that he constructed, so frail,
So barely lit, so shadowed over and nought,"
        —Wallace Stevens

After we married
You came to us precisely on time
Every Saturday for thirty-seven years.

You wore the same frown
beneath your peaked cap
Chanting your song of advice
In perfect pitch
In your dead mother's voice
When we were out of tune.
You stopped hurricanes of feeling
By mere command
And left precisely on time.

I picture you at home
Burrowing into the great books
Going to bed at nine
Wasting no time
Clipping your bachelor quarters
Like a lawn
Putting up "Keep Off" signs.

You remembered birthdays with cash
Excelled at bridge and anagrams
Chose to wake to the sound
Of your own heartbeat.

A quiet life
That shorted out the morning
You O D'd on Tylenol, plunging
Through labyrinths of mist.

How exhausting it must have been
To grow your eyes in secret
To see a door close
On the stone face of time

To travel the country of ghosts
with rocks in your throat.

THE FALL

I.

Face in the asphalt gutter
knowing my left arm shattered,

moaning, "Damn!" and "Goddamn!", police officer
over me, my life suddenly gone slack, I say

goodnight to poetry, hello insurance forms,
orthopedists, therapists, obsession with body

once again. Fallen from dailiness, bound to the gurney
by the confluence of morphine and despair,

again the turn of the wheel,
whirled into the cage of pain.

Unable to shower, dress myself, break bread,
affix a stamp, open a window, unscrew a jar,

unable to flex wrist or fingers, cast in plaster
from shoulder to thumb, I venture out.

Neighbors greet me, pretend not to see,
or grin, make jokes. "Hey, did your wife break it?"

Some tell of fatal falls,
observe cheerfully I still have two good legs.

How do I walk again on tricky ground
when the barren snows of winter come?

II.

Enter Ann G., hand therapist, convivial, merciless,
dangling resurrection of function, if I can take pain.

Sessions of silent screams—unimagined agony
as tendons, ligaments, scar tissue are wrenched

while she holds forth salon-style on sundry topics,
sculptor hands wrestling arm's flesh

as if it were putty, pausing only as I am about to faint.
When I sputter, "I forgive you, Ilse Koch," she hugs me.

Here, other pain-struck faces resemble mine.
We squint at each other through knowing eyes.

Pulleys, peg boards, iron weights, then ice
to dull the ache, anger in my throat.

Suddenly, from somewhere, nibble of a poem
stirring within me. The way back to a life.

BRAZIL'S DISPOSABLE CHILDREN

Gilberto Beto, sixteen, on the streets
of Rio since four, sorts garbage for scraps of food,
half-alive in rags, bruised by truncheons,
electric shock to fingers, anus, testicles.

"Brazil will not allow disrespect for human life,"
says the President.

Andre Leota, thirteen, on the streets
since five, eyes burned out by cigarettes,
his body stacked by police alongside others
in alleys, like cordwood, safely dead.

"One child a day is killed by death squads,"
says Amnesty International.

Marcello Pacheco, fourteen, on the streets
since eight, half-dead, force-fed cockroaches
and feces by military vigilantes.
World leaders meet at the UN Summit for Children.

"They peddle stolen car mirrors, gasoline caps,
sunglasses," says the police chief.

Nine hours from there by air,
our roses bloom. All is butter-
fat. Our children sleep
in featherbeds.

WALKING DOWN SEVENTH AVENUE

"Paranoia is a borderline
without a country on either
side."
          —Howard Moss

Ascending to the wounded sunlight
of the city
from the tomb
of Pennsylvania Station
I pass ashen men and women
curled in cartons

oblivious to the passing burst
of pedestrians
loud talk in foreign tongues
rumbling traffic and siren screams
fragments of an order
not their own.

Lives spread out on the pavement
one shoves a paper cup in my face
hoping for loose change.
Avoiding eye contact
I sidestep the gesture
charged with loss.

I recall the old days of WNYC
tolling the hour
with, "This is New York
where more than eight million people
live and work and enjoy
the fruits of democracy."

I turn from the smell of urine
of rancid bodies
extended palms of frozen ghosts

without faces   names   life histories.
I am thinking
I am not what I think I am.

Scraps of their menacing shadows
dog my footsteps. I wonder
which of them could pull a gun
flash a fist or knife to prove
I too can be humiliated.

AT THE VIETNAM VETERANS MEMORIAL

From the angle
where these two long walls meet,
the sweep of 58,000 names inscribed
white on black granite slabs
slashed into bedrock. They remain unsaid.
In the sixties, I stood on this mall
against their dying,
chanting slogans in the firestorm
of bullhorns, placards, banners.
My nerves unravel the thread
of names: July 1959 to May 1975.

Here, where two long walls meet,
east, facing the Washington Monument,
west, the Lincoln Memorial,
high polished surfaces touched
by sun's ghost
mirror clouds, lawns, bare trees
listening to winter's silence,
reflect the names on my body,
pile them inside me like snow.

At the foot of one panel,
a fresh rose and wrinkled pink paper
scrawled in pencil:
For Cpl. Dan Varner,
First Battalion, 35th Marines, Co. "C"
from your buddy, Cpl. Jan Scruggs.
I was here.

AGING AND DESERT STORM: A DUET

How many Iraqi babies will live to be old?
Why are cries of children lost on old men?
How does one grow old and remain innocent?
Why not limit soldiering to age 60 and over?

How many stiffs in the sand eaten by dogs?
Why don't we know the number of dead?
How was it like shooting fish in a barrel?
Why will the old pilot return to visit decades later?

How can the "Butcher of Baghdad" wink at us?
Why weren't smart bombs wrapped in yellow ribbon?
How does the shadow of despair lengthen with age?
Why do grand intentions come in business suits?

How do mothers wrapped in mourning black endure?
How can one hear a human voice in the metal air?

IT'S HIGH FIDELITY

if it's never failed to deliver
hasn't ever strayed in FM or AM
can go from whisper to blast
without cracking the solid state

two speakers positioned properly
are better than one—bunching sound
in ensemble more powerful than its parts
bathing the ear with hi-tech echo

as if the performers were there
in the box scattering love
into the bleakness of the day
when the dial is set just right

how human voices seem real
the lyrics infiltrating other rooms
how they demand attention and control
no fading, disengagement, or blinking

at moments of domestic friction
when lives pitch into each other
and I want to pull the plug
and hurl the damn thing out the window

A MEDITATION ON LUST

Without it we are sick
or like mad Lear cursing copulation.
The hurt father railing against appetite
even in the wren and the small gilded fly.

In our dreams, naked bodies ride
in erotic undertow like rubber rafts.
The sun paws the trees, and the turkey-cock
acclaims his hens with vulgar joy.

The huge eye of Priapus never sleeps.
Even the swollen eunuchs guarding harems
listen at doors, nursing their dark wounds,
waiting to hear cries of climax.

Boys meet secretly to masturbate
and the elderly in failing orbits
protest the separation of men from women,
perceiving the closing eye as death.

The moon leers in bedroom windows
where squeals of ecstasy are smothered
to keep from waking the children,
artifacts of lovers, hair on fire.

VISITING ETHEL

Knowing that our first glimpse of her
tied into her chair next to her bed
arrested in a perfect form of withdrawal
with blank eyes fixed on the TV
and mouthing words like wind
will trigger a numbing grief,
as if there were nothing at all
to explain

knowing she has no clue
to who we are—
Can she be glad to see us?—
you shovel ice cream into her
bloated face, body straining for release
while her querulous roommate
shrivelled and ashen, vies
for attention, eyes me
from the opposite bed, and shrieks,
"I want my mother!"

knowing I am wrong
to wish them dead—
they are, after all, free
in this dry air far beyond
our own pedagogy of pain—
still my silence is dark with anger
because they have outlived
their memories

and, knowing that after kisses
we will wave goodbye into the room
from the off-white corridor,
exchanging inane pleasantries
with the white-clad attendants,
I smother yet another impulse
to cry out in this closed box,
picturing the garden lying
in even rows beyond
the outer door.

FOR MERCE CUNNINGHAM

First a frozen brew
of dolls sprawled in space
embracing our chaos

then dislocated bodies
falling together into landscape
arms like knives
carving trees   arabesques   waves
out of air   legs moving unpredictable
free beyond logic

beyond the worry of our lives

he enters
swift small crabbed steps
time singing under his bare feet

summons couples   quartets   who come
spinning from the wings   ravel and unravel
sprout like vines in RAINFOREST

the sound of water caresses
the edge of our nerves

AT THE BALLET

"What ballet takes from life
it transforms."
                    —Balanchine

Shaping space around them with an ease
that leaves me close to tears,
I cannot believe they will grow old,
and merely human, sag and wait for death.

For now, grace and majesty of pure line
from torso to toe lifts me from the daily
through the flow of weightlessness
as I sit in darkness tied to gravity.

How can I imagine such technique built
through endless pliés at the barre, the men
beginning and ending in fifth position
after spectacular tour en l'air, the women

on point, skimming rapid-run in bourrée,
floating like silk scarves across stage,
the corps of perfect bodies intersecting
balanced in serene parabolas beyond time

as if real life were only an artifice.

HOMAGE TO TWYLA THARP
AND COMPANY

It's the way they swagger out,
lean into each other's eyes,
lofting bodies arched with love
and memory to the music of the Beach Boys.
It's the way they cuddle up in Deuce Coupe,
skitter across the floor, high
on I-don't-care impudence
while Rudner boogaloos into a turn-on.
It's the way they intersect in a fugue,
explode stomping across the stage,
eight Jelly Rolls strokin' away
in smoke house, blue-blood blues,
fanning themselves into flame.

My head bobs to alley-oop,
nerves dance, blood pounds,
foamy bones float on a river
of rhythm into the night,
blown out,
sky fresh and clear.
Arms and legs awake,
I love my body again,
a hunger deep in my gut.

PAS DE DEUX

In the dream, I move downstage
into full view of the audience I cannot see.
I am dancing toward you in half-shadow
where in white tutu
you balance in graceful arabesque...
your body a poem.
I cradle you in a lift,
but somewhere in the misted flow of movement
I falter—
I cannot tell how, or why.
Your muscles tense, I know
you have heard the scattered giggles,
the gasp or two, above the music.

When I let you down in the wings
your eyes are bleached with anger.
You slap my cheek
hiss an obscenity
in the seconds before we emerge hand in hand
to wild applause,
your rehearsed smile nourished by red roses
thrown at your feet.
They know you are not at fault.

DANCERS

Their bodies inside the music as they move
In wheels and diagonals of balance,
Their symmetry a formal garden to the eye,
They measure movement by sound,
Tutus and leotards swirling in a sea
Of shapes defining space by step.

Wings on their ankles carry dancers step
By step to our inner life to move
Us with flights of physicality. I see
with envy how ballerinas balance
In arabesque, on point, celestial sound
In the ear partnering the eye.

Would that it were I
Dancing in a pas de deux. To step
Into a lift with a ballerina to the sound
Of sensuous violins, move
Her through space in airborne balance
And set her down gently for all to see

Like a white gull descending from sky at sea.
Would that it were I
Sustaining my partner's balance
In a whirling pirouette, turned out step
A fluid detail in our dance as we move
In the spell of lighting, shadow, and sound.

My father said it was unsound
For a boy to study dance. He could see
Male dancers forgoing masculinity to move
In stylized rhythms seducing the eye
With soaring leaps, every step
Alien to normal boys in emotional balance.

But in dance, athletes and gymnasts balance
Bodies linked and leveraged, rooted in sound,
Celebrating movement as metaphor in step.
They invent new ways to see,
Teaching us how to eye
Thrust of limbs in pattern: how dancers move.

Now, I learn to balance life's daily sea
Of jarring sound against the lucid eye,
Delighting in dancers who step to music as they move.

SEVEN WAYS OF LOOKING AT A STONE

The inhuman stone rejoices.
No sensual inlays trembling
In jittery spaces.

It emits no stink.
No taste, no sound, no melting
Warmth to hoodwink

Those who lead one
On a leash, hoping
To ease being alone.

Yet, who will cast the first?
We feed on stone soup, eyeing
The bowls with distaste.

In the presence of God,
David's slingshot hurling
One at Goliath is God denied.

To see a universe
In a stone, knowing
Stones are terse

Is to leave not one
Unturned in threading
Our lives with song.

GERIATRIC WARD
(For My Father)

In the trough between the bed rails
you are coiled fetal, against the pain,
sleepless in the matrix of your coffin.
A small man in slack skin,
hands grasp through bars,
lake-blue eyes startled wide.
When they blazed, gentle would-be wife beater,
the night I held back your fists,
rare in the simmer of your manhood
I cried for you.
In the morning, you woke me with a kiss
insisting you meant well,
and left for the sweat shop
to hoist great steam irons in your callused hands.

Now, you circle your life in the blind dawn.
The others, bent over walkers,
hobble past your door like brittle couriers
diminished by bad news.
Fading appetites, the heavy treasures
of old despairs—all of it trembles.
At ninety-one, hairline fractures of small bones
are normal as shown on X-ray—
the inconceivable miracle,
the final coming to terms.

YOU MADE IT TO AMERICA

First son asleep at your breast,
you push through the Ellis Island gate,
eyes like knitting needles,
thighs ice under a heavy skirt.

Your husband, Yankee fop in vested suit,
spots you there in the crowd, lips clenched
like a fist, the brittle bond broken.
The dark hangs heavy on your back.

Hunted by Cossacks, huddled in cellars,
hands over the mouth of your two-year old.
Famine, shell bursts, a village blown open.
The stink of dead flesh.

He steps forward.
You turn away.
Anger locked in your throat.
The dark is heavy on your back.

First-born on this soil,
I tell your tale as I heard it
and lived it, jagged fragments and all,
blurred snapshots a terrible innocence.

The pushcart ghetto in Brownsville
another battleground of wills.
Stricken meals in the kitchen
of our roach-infested railroad flat.

You serve us chicken broth,
throw ashes on our hearts,
curse our names on a wind of curses.
We breathe close in our places.

I pray to be delivered from your grip,
but the first son dies at twenty-four,
and another son at five. Each time
you rock behind closed doors alone.

You tear your cheeks, merciless
in your grief. You cannot
see me. The dark hangs heavy
on your back.

You say, "Kiss me," the first, the last time
in the hospital bed where you lie dying.
I cradle you, my lips to your cheek.
"I love you," I say, wishing it were true.

The rain soaks the yews on your grave.
Did you curse them, too?
The shrivelled bushes nevergreen
died in a drought

stillborn as your fifth son
remembered in granite
across the path from your first
who sleeps in runaway ivy.

I weight your skull with a stone
to tell of my coming.

TO A TEEN-AGE DAUGHTER

Let us call a truce
and cross the sea of gall
where we have gnawed each other's flesh
infecting our lives with silence
lethal as razor-blades.
I'll forgive your platinum hair and painted eyes
if you'll stop sniping at my bi-focals
and molded shoes.

Bamboo you, scooping the air
with green finger nails
stalking my peace on stilts with nagging whine
let us sign a non-aggression pact
do away with visas when we visit
each other's rooms.

Listen.
If you will let me hold you
when we walk together
I'll consider your complaint
that I'm too old.

FATHER AND SON

Building
the body beautiful,
torso sculpted by Michelangelo,
he lifts weights & barbells
in sets of given repetitions.
Towers over me
deploring
my scrawny, pot-bellied physique
decaying with age,
his biceps thicker
than my thighs,
recommends wrist and arm curls
to start,
bench press & military press
for triceps and deltoids
to follow.

Will I study, "Physical Fitness
For Everybody" ($3.95),
go with him to the gym
in the interim?
The manual lists handgrips, leg weights,
jump ropes, slantboard, exercise wheel
to shape stomach muscles
and lower back.

We must work fast.
In a week
he's off to college upstate.

FATHER AND DAUGHTER

Every morning when I slip in
on the passenger side,
you light a cigarette,
gun the engine,
flip the dial to hard rock,
deflect my question.

Why do you let men wipe
their hands on you?
I want to say,
remembering your small shape
tucked in my arms
twenty-five years ago.
You're good enough
to be loved.
What can you do
to save your life?

Flecks of innocence
long gone,
your jet-cold eyes say,
I'll carry my grief.
You bear yours.
My life is mine to peel
or carve as I will.

Early sun spills
through the windshield
splashing your hair
with flame,
burning your baby face
into my eyes.

THYROID SURGERY

Throat slit and stapled,
swollen larynx loud with rumor,
I am left with a hoarse whisper
which could be forever.

Naked in silence,
I do not answer the telephone,
stare past acquaintances,
mouth phrases at countermen in supermarkets.

Should I learn to speak again,
what would I say?
At cocktail parties and intermissions
the clichés of small conversation,
the litanies of cunning repartee
rustle like dry leaves.

What is there to validate, confess, assert?
The talk is all self-reference
and alienation—
a crowd of voices rushing past each other.

I am responsible only for my own,
now wrapped in a cocoon—
my surgeon says, "traumatized."
In time, it will speak for itself.

Meanwhile, I carry a police whistle
to express my rage, ward off muggers,
summon relatives from a distance,
dumb amid ghosts of screaming quarrels
and carefree shouts.

SECOND LETTER TO MARION, DYING OF CANCER

Every time we meet,
the elegant bird of your body
calls for attention.
Your brassy laugh blares the music
of lamentation
edged with regret
behind the scarred surface
of yourself
as if you learned the art
of suffering
forty years ago, the day
you fell from the bike
I taught you to ride.
Twenty-six stitches,
the long shoelace tying
your face together.

We are losers all.
Each day dawns,
its light streaked
like tears.
Walking on glass,
we inch along in displays
of decorum, for reasons
no more rational than
the stone growing in your stomach.

But there is no other world.
The crocus and forsythia
you will not see again
prepare to bloom.
Sitting with legs bent beneath you
erect, voluptuous,
hazel eyes luminous
and clear past pain,
telling us to turn to one another,
you reach yourself at last.

When I said I envied you
getting off the carousel,
going to a place less stupid,
more tender than this,
I lied.

AT MEMORIAL SLOAN-KETTERING CANCER CENTER

When we walk through these doors
        we leave behind the real world.
We enter our lives, try to say
        what we feel, a geography of love
waiting to be explored.

The uniformed guard draws us in
        where fat yellow arrows on the wall
lead to Outpatient Services.
        Of the hurrying passers-by
which are the visitors? Who are the patients
        with body tumors blooming
like petaled poppies, or bloodstreams
        harboring blizzards of white cells
gone crazy?

Inside, they lie at ease
        in chemo-therapy rooms,
curative poisons seeping into their veins
        through mono-filament lines.
Some doze, others read, as transients
        peek in at them through open doors
as if they were castaways on a foreign shore.
        In Nuclear Medicine, the faces seem
to say, "We've come this far. We have
        nothing to hide," as a massive camera
scans their body's bones.
        On the 18th floor in the Breast Surgery
Rehabilitation Room, women at pulleys
        in flowered housecoats and slippers
hoist crippled arms without lymph nodes.
        From the window there, we see
the Queensboro Bridge crouched over the river
        cutting a bright path through a mix
of geometric towers. Another planet.

The first night, a blue-coated volunteer
          brings a pink rose in a bud vase.
Another one, selections of cheer
          on a book-trolley. At dawn, before bacon
and eggs—now here is a kingdom
          beyond caution—nurses arrive
for the ritual laying on of hands,
          trance-like, as if they understood
the tragedy of loss.
          How, we wonder, do they dispose
of severed breasts, limbs, organs?
          How do chaplains making their rounds
keep from being assaulted?

A MAN LEARNING WOMEN

In the breast clinic
they think he's waiting for his wife.
Then, the doctor's nurse calls his name
and he hurries in to strip
and be examined.
The women stare at each other
in disbelief.

In a circle,
a man among women hoisting arms
over mastectomies,
reaching for the edge of their pain.
What haunts him
is the terrible gift of sharing it.
What haunts them
is how he can share it—
Their fear strolling the hospital corridor
in lacy peignoirs, holding hands
with their men,
their prayer it will make no difference,
the missing side,
when a lover's hands falter.

In a circle,
nine women and a man reach up
with pullies over severed flesh.
Explore each other's eyes.
Lymph drains bang against their thighs.

His skin stretched and stitched
over rib cage
where pectoral muscle and nipple were,
he remembers cupping and tonguing
a breast.
Tactile tenderness now lost
to these women.

He's heard their soundless moans,
knows the desperate places
behind their eyes,
the quiver of hope and forced smiles
when the social worker enters
to talk prosthesis, and he leaves.

Among the one-half of one percent of men,
reluctant partner
in this circle of wounds,
he's tired of doctors' jests,
their flippant air.
Tired of pills with a woman's portrait
as logo, tired of crossing over
into their grief.

But this shared loss reeking
of bad dreams binds them.
The need to resist the stratagem
of despair.
The will to remake one's self
out of memory.

Male innocence gone, he's learned
to think like a woman.

OK, ONCE AGAIN

Clothed now and awash in cafeteria bustle
of trays, hidden among doctors and staff
in white coats reaching for the chef's special,

he passes for a visitor in the line
having taken back this day from eclipse,
catbird in the willows mewing his luck.

The day is always bright-eyed skeletons
on gurneys slipping under his skin
in elevators, corridors, and examination rooms

where he strips to be measured, thumped, re-assured
he will not soon cease to be, even with three
cancers kept at bay, one a woman's. Why not?

After the bone scan, the bloods, the x-rays,
early Korean azalea's purple blooms
dance on the lawn against the dark thing.

Soon, tulips and roses seething with hues
and the trifling quarrels composing a life,
each new start perennial fusing with sun.

MOSTLY MOZART AT PLANTING FIELDS ARBORETUM

(for Jean-Pierre Rampal)

In the great white tent lit by floodlight
And hammered by summer thundershowers
Your flute sings Mozart
To rows of upturned faces.

Beefeater frame swaying, fingers flying,
You do not see seams leak in the canvas
Overhead. Your chattering sunlight passes
Into myth, erasing all weather.

Some put up umbrellas at their seats.
I stand at the center pole drowning
In trills, runs, arpeggios.

THE GUGGENHEIM

Museum up-ended
whose skylight flows in diagonals
from top floor   down
through ceiling arches,
Kandinsky, Klee, Picasso curving   down
your spiral ramp

I list to the right,
lean toward bow-shaped benches,
archipelagoes of balance
tucked in concave corners.

Crossing to the low wall
unreeling down the helix shaft,
I curb an impulse to leap
a straight line   down
into your fish pool
in the lobby below,
wondering if Frank Lloyd Wright
really liked painting.

EIFFEL ABOVE THE CITY

He followed
the shadow drift to blue
on the rise of La Butte de Montmarte
long before we did.
Saw the silver filament of Seine
loop incandescent round
his riveted tower of lace,
his office in the sky open
only to ministers, princes, kings.

Now, hordes of tourists
lift through metal braid.
Earth drifts away as they glide
upward through wheels spinning
in a void.

Faces press against
the window of his office
where duplicated in wax
Alexander Gustave Eiffel confers
with Thomas Alva Edison.

Like smoke
from the haze of the city's
wrinkled skin below,
silence floats upward.

A POEM FOR JESSE

Raising you to my shoulder
for the obligatory burp
after four ounces of formula,
your head bobbing till I cradle it
in my palm, I begin to know again
this long-forgotten pleasure.
Worn out with lifting, carrying,
putting down a bundle of satin flesh,
I am an old man baffled by my appetite
for bonding with an eleven-week old.

Pained by the fretting,
charmed by my baptism with urine,
saddened by the harsh necessity
of our future parting,
I can't remember ever feeling so sure
about what's comic, what's tragic.

"It's hard to be a baby,"
I tell you—as you make demands
ill-understood while lying flat
on your back submitting to wet kisses.
When your stomach stutters,
or hiccups shake your tiny frame,
we mistake your grimace for a smile.
You pump your arms and legs in air
as if to assert your will,
but I fear life will teach you
how the world turns a deaf ear.

You do not love me yet, and we
have not yet spoken,
but you lock my finger in your fist
as if you care,
not minding I am over the hill
and ready to give me a second chance.
As I stand and watch you sleep,
I am loud with dreams.

SECOND POEM FOR JESSE

Even as he sits on the bedsheet spread on the floor
with teething rings, Fisher-Price toys, linen rabbits,

I am his prisoner. At seven months he remains erect
for half an hour before toppling over.

I scoop baby-food into his eager face, all mouth,
then the bottle, bliss-closed eyes as he lies

in the crook of my arm. Sleeps face down
on his stomach, tiny couch bundle covered

with a diaper for warmth, innocence as yet untouched
by loss, or the wounded planet that is his bride.

Together, we listen to music as he babbles,
beams his elfish smile, shoving into his mouth

whatever he grasps, pushing sideways in the walker
toward the sharp edges I leap to cover.

Twenty pounds now, and harder to lift, he clings
to my old bones like penetrating ointment.

Chance can murder me with his pain
as I await the world of the first tooth.

FOR MY NIECE, NITZA

Pinned down by dailiness,
almost twice your age,
I sit with you in the half-light
of a midtown bar sipping Drambuie
as you draw your map of the world,
track new roads, leaving nothing
at your back to drag you down.

You blaze the furnace of your will,
tell of heaving crates on Alaska's waterfront,
picking oranges in Israel,
hitch-hiking the African continent,
changing your name from Nancy to Nitza,
while I within the closed borders
of my aging geography live out my life
boxed in from the cold, hands frozen
to the switch of propriety.

Poised adventurer
with high brown cheekbones and tranquil eyes,
as you moved toward me across the mall
this noon, single-minded
with cat-like grace, slim-hipped,
strong shoulders bare in a summer dress
flaring like a lily,
I could see nobody owns you.

D-O-G
(for Albie Sachs)

Usual morning ritual
leaving the car door open
as you turn the ignition key.

The blast tears off your right arm,
blinds your right eye,
shrapnel peppers scalp, chest, feet.

South African forget-me-not you knew
was coming after the letter-bomb killed
Ruth First, Dulcie September shot dead.

Assassin hounds of apartheid
dogged you to Mozambique in exile,
detonated your stubborn torso.

"D-o-g"...In a hospital in Britain
you slowly write the letters, "d-o-g"
over and over to train the left hand.

"D-o-g"...25 years of doggedness in courtrooms
defending blacks. Solitary confinement. Still
won't bend at 53. They can't teach an old dog...

The nurse comes in with pain-killers
and your copy of JAIL DIARY.
She checks the corridors, stairwell.

THE NEW WISDOM

Holed up in my room
my heart pounds
and panic flows from my blood
when a siren cries in the night.
On the street I still check back over my shoulder
every few steps.

In those naked dawns
when I lay in my cage
throwing up from the pain
praying for death
trainees came to see the ghost of me.
I kissed their boots when they laughed.

Face it.
Principles will kill you faster than cancer.
Countless fools on parapets
have been ground through the teeth of the state.
To live unnoticed is best—
feeding on bread and circuses.

HOW *NOT* TO THINK ABOUT
NUCLEAR WAR

Jog three miles rinsed in sweat
limbs alive to wind. Shower,
make love.

Tumble with your son.
Tickle his peachbud skin.
Mimic babybirds. A lion in the veldt.

Walk the city by night.
Capture that luminous hour
before dawn.

Explore orchids in the green house.
Discover some reason in the rhythm
of petals.

Play a Bach chaconne
on the stereo.
Listen.

Fly east to London, Paris, Amsterdam.
Try sleeping when sunrise lifts
in the plane window.

Eat. Pasta, chocolates, snails.
Gorge yourself. Food consoles
like time.

Visit the famous dead
in cemeteries. Consider how their slipshod
legends wax and wane.

Mourn with care. The heart's ice
will drag you down. Scorn grief's excess
as another way of being alone.

Live hard. Leave yourself free
for laughter. Hang on, even if it's a lie
you've told yourself.